I0472553

Book 1
Acrylic Painting
By Scott Landowski

&

Book 2
Pastel Drawing
By Scott Landowski

Book 1
Acrylic Painting

By Scott Landowski

1-2-3 Easy Techniques To Mastering Acrylic Painting!

Acrylic Painting: 1-2-3 Easy Techniques To Mastering Acrylic Painting!

Copyright 2017 by Scott Landowski - All rights reserved.

In no way is it legal to reproduce, duplicate, or transmit any part of this document in either electronic means or in printed format. Recording of this publication is strictly prohibited and any storage of this document is not allowed unless with written permission from the publisher. All rights reserved.

Table of Contents

Introduction

I want to thank you and congratulate you for downloading the book, "Acrylic Painting: 1-2-3 Easy Techniques to Mastering Acrylic Painting!"

This book contains proven steps and strategies on how to become an expert in creating simply wonderful artworks with the use of acrylic paints, and with the aid of easy-to-follow tips and advice on the different techniques involved in acrylic painting.

As a beginner in the world of acrylic painting, you probably already have some ideas about the craft, which is what enticed you to try it in the first place. But getting your act together and apply what you have learned can be challenging. It can be quite intimidating too; and this is what this book aims to help you with.

The information contained in this book will help you appreciate the beauty of using acrylics, as well as the versatility that they allow you to enjoy. You can use acrylics in more ways than you can imagine. You will learn to create many different effects that are surprisingly easy to execute and yet allow you to turn out amazing (and complex) works of art.

Simply follow the instructions contained here and you will be on your way to making your very own acrylic masterpieces.

Thanks again for downloading this book. I hope you enjoy it!

Chapter 1. Fully Armed: Gathering The Proper Painting Supplies

Acrylic painting can serve as a productive way to pass the time. It is also a good way to put your artistic skills to good use. Moreover, it is a wonderful way of creating art that you can share to your family and friends. You will surely have a great time experimenting with acrylic painting, so long as you have the proper materials.

PAINT

1. Select the kind of acrylic paint to work with.

There is a lot of acrylic paint for you to choose from. You can easily get confused trying to choose between different brands, especially since acrylic paint also comes in jars or tubes. The important thing to remember when it comes to purchasing your acrylic paint is that you may well be better off buying the more expensive ones.

Cheaper brands of acrylic paints might seem budget-friendly, but you will actually end up spending more if you buy them. They contain fewer pigments than the pricier ones, which means you will have to use more of them to achieve the vibrant colors you desire.

2. Go for the most basic when choosing your colors.

It would be wise to begin acrylic painting by using the most basic of colors. You can then easily come up with other colors by mixing the basic ones. It is also important that you do not get carried away when purchasing your colors; one tube or jar of each of the following should be enough: phthalo blue, cadmium red, azo yellow medium, phthalo green, burnt umber, Payne's gray, and titanium white.

3. Consider acrylic paint that comes in tubes.

As a beginner, it might be better to use using paint that comes in tubes. Starting out with smaller amounts of paint can help you avoid wasting too much money on unused paint. Moreover, the quality of acrylic paint that is contained in a jar is in no way different from that found inside a tube.

BRUSH

1. Buy the best paint brushes your budget allows.

Because paintbrushes come in a wide array of brands, styles, shapes, and sizes, deciding what to buy can easily make you feel overwhelmed. But what is great about acrylic painting is that the paint (medium) you are working with is water-based, which allows you to use any and all of these brushes. Be careful to choose brushes that are specifically for acrylic painting, however; you can actually use those brushes that are designed for use in oil painting (which also come with longer handles and stiffer bristles), but those that are intended for watercolor (which are designed to have short handles and soft bristles) will not do.

You will find that acrylic paint brushes are made from either animal hair (mink/sable, squirrel, or hog) or synthetic fibers; other brushes are made out of a mix of these two materials. To guarantee your success with acrylic painting, go for synthetic brushes that are made of the highest quality materials. Acrylic paint can be quite damaging to your brushes: they dry quickly and bind to the bristles, causing the latter to easily lose their shape.

2. Know that size matters in choosing paint brushes.

One thing to keep in mind when choosing your acrylic paint brushes is that the bigger the brush head's size, the higher the paint handle's number will be. Different brush manufacturers do not follow the same sizing, which is why you can buy a certain brand of 12-inch brush that is slightly bigger than another 12-inch brush from another brand. To keep things simple, remember that a 12-inch flat brush's head generally has a width of about one inch.

Speaking of how size matters in choosing your acrylic paintbrushes, you should buy them while keeping the size of your painting in mind. If you know that you are definitely going to create a large artwork with no fussy details, then buying a small brush may not be your best bet. Using the wrong-sized paintbrush is the easiest path to becoming bored and frustrated with acrylic painting.

3. Identify the different kinds of paintbrushes.

Paintbrushes that are most commonly used in acrylic painting are the following:

Flat brush. A flat brush comes with a flat ferrule, which is the metal piece that keeps the medium to long brush hairs in place. What makes a flat brush essential to acrylic painting is its ability to hold a big amount of paint, letting you create wider marks when you use the side as well as thinner marks when you use the tip. A flat brush is also useful for painting an object's planes.

Filbert brush. A Filbert brush is similar to the flat brush in that it also has a flat ferrule, but this one is thicker and comes with long hairs that are oval-shaped. You can use this brush to blend your acrylic paint with ease.

Round brush. A round brush, with its round ferrule as well as its pointy tip, is a great tool to use in adding details to your painting. You can also use it to apply fills, to vary the thickness of the lines you draw, and to execute the washing technique *(you can skip to Chapter 3 for details)*.

Fan brush. Use a fan brush (which has brush hairs that are spread in a fan shape and that are held together by a flat ferrule) to blend your acrylic colors as well as to create special painting effects.

Liner brush. The thin liner brush, with its long brush hairs coming to a point out of its round ferrule, is great for creating linear details in your painting – and for finishing off the latter with your signature.

Angular brush. An angular brush is another brush that also comes with a flat ferrule, but this one has an angles brush shape. You will find this particular brush quite useful in drawing curves and lines, for creating details, and for working into corners.

Bright brush. Bright brushes are a bit similar to flat brushes due to their flat ferrules, but their hairs are shorter, giving you more control when making shorter strokes and when using thicker acrylic paint.

PALETTE

1. Choose the palette that suits your taste.

It is important that you choose a palette with the same care that you put into choosing your acrylic colors. A palette is what you need for mixing paint on, and you can even use it to house your paint in between sessions. A plastic or paper plate can serve as an inexpensive palette; what you are looking for is something that is flat and wide, and that has a clean surface.

When finding a palette to work with, it helps to also find a water-filled spray bottle to accompany it. Acrylic paint tends to dry quickly, and you can avoid this dilemma by simply spraying your paint with water to help it stay moist.

2. Consider buying a palette that retains moisture.

Squeezing acrylic paint onto your palette can cause it to dry even before you have used it all up. This is why it would be wise for you to consider buying a palette that has a moisture-retaining feature. A moisture-retaining palette (also called a stay-wet palette) comes with a say-wet paper as well as a wet sponge to keep your acrylic paint from drying up and to make it workable for a long time.

3. Buy a palette knife and cups as well.

You will find several small cups useful in acrylic painting, especially if you are going to be mixing large amounts of paint at the same time. You can use them to store your paint until the next painting session, which is a better way of preserving your acrylic paint compared to wrapping your palette in plastic.

Meanwhile, instead of using your paintbrush to mix acrylics on your palette, you can use a palette knife to avoid wasting your paint (a lot can stay stuck in your brush). Aside from helping you mix colors easily, a palette knife also lets you effortlessly scrape off paint (if it is still moist) on your canvas in case you make mistakes.

CANVAS

1. Choose your blank slate.

Deciding what surface to work on is another important thing you have to take into account when painting with acrylics. The fact that acrylic paint is on the heavy, thick side means you don't really have too many surfaces to work on. Most people who paint with acrylics usually use canvas boards, stretched canvas, treated wood, or watercolor paper. Just make sure that you don't paint on anything that is too porous, oily, or greasy.

2. Consider practicing on paper first.

You can't expect yourself to paint up an acrylic masterpiece each time you take up your paintbrush, especially when as a beginner; you are still trying to get the hang of acrylic painting. This is the reason you have to constantly practice. Playing with your acrylics on paper lets you so this without wasting too much money on canvas, and also gets rid of the issue of where to store your practiced-on canvas. You might consider practicing on a large sketchbook that is wire-bound. Or you can always get yourself a pad's worth of paper that is textured like canvas.

3. Know that more is better.

Consider going for a canvas that has been pre-stretched and primed. Using this type of canvas provides you more time doing acrylic art. It would also be best to buy several pre-stretched, primed canvas in various shapes and sizes (your landscapes will turn out better when done on long, thin canvas).

SMALL ITEMS

1. Get a pair of fingerless gloves for your hands.

Wearing fingerless gloves is a great way of keeping your hands warm as your fingertips work on gripping your paintbrush. Choose a pair that is made from a stretchy material (like a cotton/lycra blend) for a comfortably snug fit that allows for plenty of movement and does not hinder you from painting.

2. Buy water containers for your brushes and paints.

A container is useful for holding water that you need to wash and rinse our paintbrushes, as well as for thinning your acrylic paint. You could go for a simple glass jar, but a plastic container that will not easily break when dropped might be a better option. Consider purchasing different kinds of containers. It would also be a good idea to buy a container that comes with holes along its edges, and then store your paintbrushes in it to dry.

3. Cover up with rags.

Rags are good for removing excess paint from your brushes, as well as for ensuring that you get rid of most of the acrylic paint before you clean them. You can also use paper towels, old sheets, torn shirts, or any other fabric material that has not been tainted with any kind of cleanser or moisturizer (this is to avoid anything from contaminating your acrylic paint.

You should not forget to also cover yourself up with an old, oversized shirt or a smock to protect your clothes from acrylic stains. And remember to have several sheets of old newspapers laid on your tabletops in order to avoid huge clutter.

Chapter 2. All Prepped Up: Things To Do Before You Start Painting

Another thing that makes acrylic painting such a great hobby to learn and indulge in is the fact that it allows you to produce quality artwork in vibrant colors that is similar to that you can create with oil painting, minus the time and expense that oil painting requires.

You have to keep the following things in mind, however, to ensure turning out great artworks even if you are still a beginner in acrylic painting:

SETTING, SUPPLIES, AND SUBJECT

1. Select your setting.

The right location is essential in painting, whether you do it with acrylics or another medium. A setting that allows for natural light is best for doing your painting in. You can achieve such setting by making sure to set up your work station beside an open window that lets in plenty of natural light. Doing so will let you pick out any mistakes (issues with gradation of colors, for example – *see Chapter 4 for a more detailed explanation on the subject of gradation*) that you would not have noticed under the wrong setting.

2. Put your acrylic painting supplies in place.

The next thing to do after you have picked out the perfect location is to get your acrylic painting supplies all laid out. It would be best for you to arrange them in such a way that makes you feel the most comfortable and that helps you do your work efficiently. Pour water into your containers, lay out all the paints and paintbrushes that you are going to use, and set your painting palette where you think is the most ideal. It also helps if you wear your good old shirt or smock this time.

3. Choose your painting subject.

Then decide on the subject you are going to be working on. For your first foray into the world of acrylic painting, the easiest route for you to take would be to paint from a photograph or a 3D object; trying to put a picture on your mind onto your canvas can more than likely be difficult at this stage. If you are having a hard time coming up with a painting subject, you can always consider these easy ones: knickknacks around your house, a bowl overflowing with fruits, a view of the sunset, or a vase filled with beautiful flowers in bloom.

PAINTING SURFACE

1. Prep your canvas first.

Getting your canvas prepped up is an important task you have to do prior to painting. As mentioned in *Chapter 1 in relation to choosing your canvas*, you can never go wrong with starting out with a primed painting surface; you will do even better if you use a small one. Keep in mind that you need to sand your canvas lightly before you begin painting. After sanding (fine-tooth sanding paper would be better than a coarse-grade one for this job), wipe its surface with a soft, clean cloth.

2. Decide on whether to paint directly on your canvas or to cover it with a neutral color first.

You have a choice between painting directly onto your primed (applied with Gesso) canvas's white surface or prepping your canvas first with neutral gray. As you continually practice on your acrylic painting, you can then try prepping your canvas with brighter colors.

Going with painting directly on white canvas allows you to have a pure looking and more bright tone, although you will have to use more acrylic paint to cover your canvas. If you do decide on prepping your canvas with a neutral gray, take some black paint as well as some Titanium white paint. Mix the two paints until you get a color that appears to be medium gray (make sure the quantity is enough to cover your whole canvas in one go).

To prep your canvas: Spritz the canvas lightly with water before using your paintbrush to smooth the water over in order to lightly dampen its entire surface. You may then brush the gray paint over the entire surface of your canvas to evenly cover it, after which the canvas should be allowed to dry.

3. Draw a rough sketch on your canvas.

As a beginner in acrylic painting, you might not be too confident in your painting skills yet, and this is why it may be best for you to first make an outline, from which you can let your paintbrush follow along. You may use any kind of pencil to roughly sketch your subject's outline onto the canvas; during this stage, you don't have to think about putting in details yet.

You can either roughly sketch your outline right onto the canvas by freehand or by tracing. If you are going for the second option, you need to measure your tracing paper first to make sure that its size is similar to that of your canvas. Use tape to secure the tracing paper over your canvas, and then carefully insert a sheet of transfer paper (wax-free) between the tracing paper and the canvas. Use a colored pencil to lightly go over your sketch lines, and then check if your lines have been transferred onto the canvas.

PAINT MIXING

1. Make sure that your paints stay moist.

Take a dinner plate that you will not be using anymore (a paper plate works as well) so you have something to squeeze your acrylic paints onto. It helps if you place a damp paper towel on the plate, as this will keep them workable for a longer time. You may also have to add a little water to your paints as you squeeze them out of their tubes, as they are somewhat creamy and thick.

2. Mix all your paints before painting.

A mistake commonly made by beginners in acrylic painting is to mix their paints as they work, when they actually need to do the mixing before they start painting. Mixing all the acrylic colors you are going to be working with before starting to paint allows you to use your paints as well as your time with efficiency. To be on the safe side, mix more acrylic paints than you think you will need. Although you can refer to a color wheel in mixing your acrylic paints, it might be difficult at first to come up with the exact paint shade twice. Besides, you can always store the extra paints for future use.

The important thing to remember when mixing your paints is to combine red, yellow, and blue (primary colors) to come up with basic colors, and to combine primary and secondary colors to turn out more specific colors. In case you find it impossible to get the shade you want from your limited paint palette, there is a wide array of acrylic colors you can choose from in art supply stores.

3. Know how to mix paints properly.

Mixing your acrylic colors is a straightforward process: using your palette knife, simply combine your colors and then mix. Once you get the hang of color mixing, however, you can move on to more creative ways of doing it. For example, you can choose to partially mix your acrylic paints before working (use your palette knife to give your paints a quick mix, and you will get interesting color blends that will look wonderful on your canvas), or create a family of tones (having a variety of pink shades or skin tones, for instance, can help you easily paint understated variances).

Chapter 3. Lights, Paintbrush, Action: Paint Away!

First things first: Choosing your light source before painting creates a huge impact on how your acrylic colors – and your painting – will turn out. Your acrylic colors can change with how light hits them, which is why you need to locate your primary source of light prior to painting. It is also important to see to it that you paint your lighter colors near the light source and to have your darker colors at a distance.

Once you have decided on your light source, you are ready.

GETTING STARTED

1. Inspect your subject's composition.

Even if you only have a single painting subject in mind, you have to layer it with other backgrounds or surfaces. After examining your subject, identify the details that are nearest to you or furthest from you. You also have to pay attention to texture, color changes, and overlapping, all of which you will try to recreate in your painting.

2. Start painting by doing the background.

After carefully looking over your painting subject, you can then start painting the background on your canvas. The important thing to keep in mind when painting is to layer upwards, which means that you should paint from the back first before doing the front. Begin painting with the medium value colors, and then work on the darkest ones. Do the brightest colors last, after which you can build up your basic colors as well as add in your details in the background. You need to add light points and shadows if a solid color makes up your background; if it is busy or patterned, you should complete the layer by adding movement and texture with several strokes of your brush.

3. Carefully paint in your subject's shapes.

As you start painting your subject, you have to see to it that it gets broken up into identifiable shapes, which you will need to paint in solid colors. You will see that your subject will start appearing as you build up your subject's colors and shapes. To help make the process of painting a little less challenging, paint in small areas at a time. You might try using a grid system to make the painting of your subject a bit easier: Imagine that your canvas is split into parts, and then work on a grid space at a time. Keep in mind that medium value colors should be added first; add the darker colors next before finishing off with the lighter ones. This will help make the layering of your colors much easier (it will be difficult to paint a lighter color over a dark one).

Once you have painted your basic shapes and colors, it is now time to add your subject's details with the help of certain techniques

ACRYLIC PAINTING TECHNIQUES

1. Consider dry brush and washing applications.

Dry brush. You will find that using a dry paintbrush in applying your acrylic paints (undiluted) to your canvas will let you create strokes of strong colors. The lack of water will give you hard edges and uneven lines, but you can make use of these features to lend movement and texture to your painting.

Washing. What is great about using acrylic paints is that, by diluting them with the right amount of water, you can use them the way you would watercolors *(you will find a round brush helpful with this technique; see Chapter 1 for details)*. If you water down your paint, you can give your canvas a translucent wash. The advantage of using acrylic paint over watercolor to apply this technique is that the effect will be permanent. If you mix the washing method with the dry brush technique, you will find that it will help you create different textures in your painting.

2. Make use of your palette knife and paper towel.

Palette knife. You can make your acrylic painting as artsy as it can get with the aid of your palette knife. Just use it to scrape up a little paint, and then apply on your canvas. When applying the paint, you can make believe that you are buttering bread or frosting cake in an artful way.

Paper towel. Meanwhile, you can try your hand at "sponge painting": simply dab on color accents on your painting with the help of the corner of a clean sponge or paper towel. This technique is quite helpful in capturing the movement and texture of tress as they sway in a breeze.

3. Try detailing, stippling, and flicking with your paintbrush.

Detailing. You can use a fine brush to add in the glisten on a bird's wings, the whites of your human subject's eyes, or other small details.

Stippling. Stippling is a great method to use in your painting. It lets you create a group of fine dots that show subtle color variations to produce textured images as well as moving scenes.

Flicking. To create the effect of an uneven splatter on your canvas, you can flick your acrylic paint with the use of a wet brush. Flicking is a wonderful way of creating a starry night or adding texture to your abstract landscape.

Acrylic Painting: 1-2-3 Easy Techniques To Mastering Acrylic Painting!

BRUSH TECHNIQUE PROBLEMS

Speaking of using your paintbrush as a form of acrylic painting technique, here are some tips on dealing with brush technique problems.

1. Working with the brush technique takes up too much time.

To get around the issue of the brushing technique taking up too much of your time, it would be best for you to use the biggest brush possible. If you use a brush that is appropriately-sized for your painting, you are assured that the process will be more efficiently carried out. A large brush will help you work on more portions of your canvas at a faster rate. Moreover, the longer you use a bigger brush, the higher your chances of improving in acrylic painting. You will be able to explore acrylic painting in many ways as you learn how to control your paintbrush. And because you are not changing brushes that often, you will find it easier to maintain your momentum in painting.

2. Working with the brush technique is not easy.

Once you understand what the different functions of a paintbrush are, you will find it easier to use it in the acrylic painting brush technique:

For scooping up your acrylic paint. How much acrylic paint can be held by your paintbrush depends on its size as well as the type of its bristles. For example, you can utilize a big paintbrush that comes with strong bristles like a trowel in scooping up huge amounts of acrylic paint. Its bristles are strong enough to pick up undiluted paint. Meanwhile, a smaller brush with soft bristles is useful in holding acrylic paint that has been thinned.

For creating watercolor effects. Acrylic paint needs to be diluted (thinned) with water to make it penetrate your paintbrush. In the case of creating watercolor effects, use a brush that comes with soft bristles to allow your diluted acrylic paints to "flow."

For controlling the outcome of your painting. Simply changing the pressure with which you hold your paintbrush can help you control how it behaves on your canvas. If you apply the right amount of pressure, you will find that the shape of your paintbrush becomes less important than the stiffness of its bristles.

3. Working with the brush technique makes for a sloppy artwork.

A common challenge that beginners in acrylic painting experience, especially when they attempt to do it with a bigger paintbrush, is being able to make brush strokes on canvas with a "feather touch." You yourself might find it difficult to make the smooth transition from using your brush to apply paint the way a house painter would paint your home, to a more discreet and gentle manner as you apply acrylic paint on your canvas, especially in working on a more detailed painting.

Acrylic Painting: 1-2-3 Easy Techniques To Mastering Acrylic Painting!

To help you turn out wonderful effects in your acrylic painting, consider following this exercise in subtle painting, which requires you to use very small amounts of acrylic paint on your brush as well as an extremely soft approach:

1. Take a size 12 paintbrush; make sure that it is completely dry. Dip its tip into your acrylic paint (undiluted), and then flick off as much as paint as you can from the brush so that only a very small amount of paint is left on it.

2. Apply the paintbrush holding the tiny amount of paint on your canvas, seeing to it that you use only a small amount of pressure. Doing it this way lets your brush work on the highest parts of your canvas only. You will notice that the less amount of paint there is on your paintbrush, the more areas there are on your canvas that your brush passes. This technique, when used with a single feather-light sweep, is useful in adding texture to an extremely flat surface.

3. Add a small amount of water or thinner to your acrylic paint. Using your paintbrush's tip with a light hand, repeat the second step. You will see that you have just painted in seagrass on your canvas. Using this technique also allows you to recreate images of the sunlit tips of grass as well as of sand dunes.

Chapter 4. Groundwork: Techniques To Use In Making Your Painting Come To Life

Turning out a flat-looking painting is something you would not want to happen, especially after all the hard work you have painstakingly put into it. To help you make your acrylic painting subject come to life, consider the following:

BUILDING TECHNIQUES

1. Under painting

Under painting lets you have flashes of a contrasting color showing through in your canvas, which makes for an interesting effect. To shake things up a bit, you could go for an unexpected under painting color. For example, if your subject is mostly green, you can use a vibrant red color for your under painting. To begin this technique, use paint in a color that contrasts wonderfully with your finished painting's palette to roughly sketch your chosen image. You can then use opaque acrylic to paint over your under painting to hide traces of paint underneath, or allow parts of it to shine through to create a dimensional effect.

2. Glazing

The glazing technique involves diluting your acrylic paints and applying them thinly on your canvas. You have the option of making your glaze as simple or as complicated as you want. Although there are plenty of additives that you can choose from in order to create your glaze, you can always use plain water.

You have to keep in mind, however, that your acrylic paints are basically made with glue that has been incorporated with lots of colored grit. The larger the amount of water you add to your paints, the more likely their glue component is going to break down. If you go overboard in diluting your paints, you will end up working with a glaze that is difficult to work with. If you try painting over the over-diluted glaze, you risk removing it in the process.

3. Layering

Either the under painting or glazing method of building your painting can be combined with the layering technique. The key is to work in layers, which means that you have to build your painting by starting at the bottom. You need to begin the layering process by painting huge color blocks, which you can accomplish with washes, before adding more details as you keep adding on layers. An easy way to execute the layering technique is to make a tracing of your subject first, making sure that each color is separated into separate shapes. You can then create your monochromatic palette (or a palette of varied colors) before painting in your subject's shapes in the same way that you would work on a do-it-yourself paint-by-numbers painting.

There is actually another way of giving more life to a rather flat painting, and that is through the creation of texture. Lending some texture to your painting, especially if you do it in a way that allows certain areas that are highly textured to pop out against other areas that are rather flat, lets you give it an interesting contrast as well as a new dimension.

CREATING TEXTURE

Now, you can definitely create texture in your painting with a paintbrush, but know that you can use plenty of other materials to accomplish the same thing. You can take a piece of cardboard, a discarded credit card, or anything that can be used to apply paint.

1. Glue it down or trowel it on.

An easy and fun way of giving texture to your acrylic painting is to attach, by gluing it down, a fitting literature with a bit of a binder medium. You can then add about 3 to 4 dense coats of good quality impasto gel before adding a wash or glaze as well. Afterwards, you can paint an image over the top, something that has relevance to the text underneath, and that will let said text show through in certain areas. You could also try troweling on a bit of modeling compound, and then pushing into its surface certain objects or shapes. Either way, your painting will get plenty of wonderful texture.

2. Stencil it in.

It would also be a great idea to use stencils as a means of creating texture in your painting. You can lay lace, for instance, on your painting's surface before adding a good layer of impasto gel (clear). Once the gel has dried, get a paintbrush and then drag it across the top; soon you will see the pattern being revealed.

3. Add anything that suits your fancy.

You can let your imagination run wild to come up with fancy, quirky, or odd materials to add to your painting and give it the texture it needs – old car tires, dirt, sand, and gravel are welcome.

Now, a painting that looks like it has come to life can only be achieved if the acrylic colors appear seamless, which is why an exercise in gradation is in order. But what is gradation? It simply refers to the act of smoothly blending your acrylic colors so that any transition point between could not be seen. Letting your colors go from blue to white is not an example of gradation, but having your colors shift smoothly through three shades of blue is, and you will be able to do the same once you master this. The following exercises will help:

GRADATION EXERCISE: Blending Acrylic Colors

Materials: Paint palette (large), canvas (or any primed painting surface), water pot (large), white acrylic paint, and phthalo blue paint (or one in your favorite color).

Directions:

1. Draw some chalk lines that will let your manage your palette colors well. For someone like you who is still new to acrylic painting, drawing columns with your chalk would be sufficient.

2. After drawing in your chalk lines, you can then paint the color you have decided on at the highest point in your palette's column (for example, you should fill the warm red column with warm red paint, and the cool blue column with the cool blue paint. Make sure to apply paint broadly on the canvas. Meanwhile, mix in white paint to your color on the palette, and then apply it in the column underneath the first color, making sure that you create a broad line. Use your paintbrush to pull your two colors together, seeing to it that whoever is viewing the painting will find it hard to tell exactly where the lighter color starts and the darker color ends.

3. Repeat the process described in the second step until you reach the bottom where the pure white paint is. To prevent this pure white section from being tainted with any other color in your paintbrush, thoroughly clean your paintbrush before dipping it into white paint.

Once you have the process of blending your acrylic colors down pat (you can practice on a small area of your "training" canvas board), you can then move on to this next exercise, which involves mixing your acrylic colors together on the canvas:

GRADATION EXERCISE: Mixing Acrylic Colors

Materials: Canvas (or any primed painting surface), paint palette (large), water pot (large), phthalo blue paint, titanium white paint, cadmium yellow light paint, and paintbrush (large, size 10/12).

Directions:

1. Have a large and sturdy water pot (filled with water, of course) by the side of your extremely large paint palette. Then draw several vertical chalk lines on your canvas. Take the palette, as well as a big paintbrush (choose one in size 10 or size 12), and start dropping a blob of blue acrylic paint in the column right below the blue (you can add more paint if you did not scoop up enough the first time. Mix well before adding a bit of a light yellow color as well as a bit of white color. Mix these three colors together, making sure to keep them in the blue column.

You will find that doing this gradation exercise, in which you have to use more than one color, can be quite a challenge. Just keep in mind that you have to completely mix your different colors so that you will no longer see pure color flecks remaining.

2. After coming up with a wonderful turquoise blue color from doing the first step, you can now use that color on your canvas. Make sure to scoop up a lot of the color on your brush and then apply it on the canvas using a crosshatch pattern. In case you notice any holes showing through and you find yourself having to scrub your paint on, this only means that you have not mixed an adequate amount of paint. You will have to mix more blue, light yellow and white paints in order to come up with more of the turquoise blue color you need.

3. Now it is time for you to take another dollop of blue paint (lesser in amount this time) and as a bigger dollop of light yellow paint. Add in a bigger dollop of white paint as well and then mix right beneath the first color mix you came up with. The color this time should turn out paler and "yellower" in appearance. Apply this color mix to your canvas, making sure to blend it carefully to your first color mix with the use of the crosshatch technique.

Use the same crosshatch technique in creating bands of color to pull all your colors together. Repeat the process as you go down within the chalk lines you have made, adding more and more quantities of light yellow and white. This will give you much paler and "yellower-er" colors – and your painting will have a beautiful ocean-like image.

Chapter 5. Picture Perfect: Finishing Touches To Make To Your Painting

Once you have finished your painting and are allowed it to dry completely, it is a good idea to apply a layer of varnish to it as a final touch. This is a particularly wise thing to do if you are not planning on framing your painting under glass, in order to protect it from dust, dirt, and environmental pollutants. Varnishing your painting also gives it an evened-out appearance (either equally matte or glossy).

The type of varnish to use on your painting

You have the option of giving your acrylic painting a glossy finish (when a gloss varnish dries, you get a completely clear finish) or a matte finish (a matte/satin finish lends a faint appearance of frosted glass), which you can apply with the use of a brush or by spraying the varnish straight out of the can. It is important that you check your varnish bottle's label to make sure that it can be easily removed in the future, in case it eventually becomes discolored and needs to be replaced with a new layer of varnish.

The right time to varnish your painting

It is essential that your painting dries completely before you apply your varnish, since doing otherwise might make the varnish trap moisture, turn cloudy, and crack. You may have to wait for as long as six weeks to make sure that your acrylic colors are fully dried all throughout. Once you are completely sure that your painting has thoroughly dried, then you can varnish.

What to do before varnishing your painting: Aside from seeing to it that your painting is completely dry, you also have to ensure that no dust has settled on its surface. When your painting is dust-free, you can rest assured that the varnish you apply on it will flow evenly, leaving no unsightly brush marks behind (which can also be remedied by diluting the varnish as well as using a brush specially designed for the job). To get rid of any grease, dirt, and dust, lay your painting flat before slightly dampening it with a cotton wool soaked in clean water; use another cotton wool to dry your painting; manually remove any fibers of cotton that might have stuck to the painting; and allow the painting to dry overnight by leaning it against one wall, with its face inward.

Now, you can start:

VARNISHING YOUR ACRYLIC PAINTING

1. Get a flat-bristle painting brush.

It is best to apply your varnish using a brush with a flat bristle. Lay your acrylic painting flat, and then varnish from top to bottom. Apply the varnish from one edge to the other in parallel strokes, and make sure to work in one direction the whole time. Once the varnish has dried, you can apply another coat. Make sure to work at right angles to your first coat so that you end up with an even finish.

2. Let your varnished painting dry.

Once you are done varnishing your painting, you have to lay it flat for ten minutes or more. This will prevent the applied varnish from running down your painting. After ten minutes, you can then prop your finished painting against one wall to let it dry with its face inwards. Because acrylic paints need to cure, you have to keep your painting in a place where it will not be disturbed for one to two days. How to know that your painting's varnish has dried? Simply touch the painting's edge; if it is no longer tacky, then it is already dry.

3. Keep these tips in mind:

It is extremely important that you varnish your entire painting in one sitting. Doing one area at a time will mean that one part will dry earlier than the others, and this will leave noticeable lines on your painting. You also have to make sure that your brush uses the same quantity of varnish with each stroke; otherwise your finished painting will have an uneven appearance. And remember to work in somewhere that is not dusty (to avoid getting dust particles stuck in varnish that is still wet) and where no cats are around (to prevent potential paw prints from showing up in your finished painting).

Meanwhile, after all is said and done, you have to do these:

3 THINGS TO DO AFTER YOU HAVE FINISHED YOUR PAINTING

1. Wipe off or paint over your mistakes.

If you notice some sort of mistake in your painting, you can just wipe the oversight off using a dampened rag (make sure it has been washed and is dust-free). You can also paint over your mistake once your painting has thoroughly dried. If painting over is too much of a challenge, you can always just white-out your error by using Gesso (a painting canvas primer) and paint again on that area.

2. Wash, wipe, and save.

Cleaning your paintbrushes after each painting session is a must. Any bits of acrylic paint that are left on your brushes can damage them, especially when they are left to dry on the bristles. Use cold water (hot or warm water will cause the acrylic paint to set in your paintbrushes) and soap to wash your brushes. After letting the water run clear, you can then move on to cleaning your work space, wiping up any paints on surfaces and rinsing the jars you used with water.

You should also make the effort to save any of your unused paints. If you place your acrylic paints in airtight containers, you can make them last for a number of months until your next painting session. Aside from scooping your paints into containers with airtight lids, you can also seal them into your moisture-retaining palette *(as previously suggested in Chapter 1).*

3. Strut your stuff.

And rightfully so. An artwork is meant to be seen by other people, so put your acrylic painting on display. Whether you just hang your painting as it is or have it framed first, showcase it in your house so friends or family can see it, or just so you'll have something that can serve as a reminder of what you are capable of creating.

Conclusion

Thank you again for downloading this book!

I hope this book enabled you to realize that although dabbling in acrylic painting can seem nerve-racking at first, there are plenty of tips and advice you can follow to easily get over those nerves. Hopefully, this book has taught you that acrylic painting is truly fun!

The next step is to get as creative as you possibly can. Following the techniques given in this book is a must, but it does not mean that you must box yourself within those guidelines. Once you have mastered the various methods in acrylic painting, there is no reason why you should not explore other means of using acrylics to come up with unique pieces of art. The key is to practice – and then to practice a lot more.

Finally, if you enjoyed this book, please take the time to share your thoughts and post a review on Amazon. It'd be greatly appreciated!

Thank you and good luck!

Book 2
Pastel Drawing

By Scott Landowski

1-2-3 Easy Techniques To Mastering Pastel Drawing

Pastel Drawing: 1-2-3 Easy Techniques To Mastering Pastel Drawing

Copyright 2017 by Scott Landowski - All rights reserved.

In no way is it legal to reproduce, duplicate, or transmit any part of this document in either electronic means or in printed format. Recording of this publication is strictly prohibited and any storage of this document is not allowed unless with written permission from the publisher. All rights reserved.

Table of Contents

Introduction

I want to thank you and congratulate you for downloading the book, "Pastel Drawing: 1-2-3 Easy Techniques to Mastering Pastel Drawing!"

This book contains proven steps and strategies on how to master the pastel medium to create stunning works of art. Art, in all its forms, plays an essential role in making our everyday lives more delightful, satisfactory and inspirational. It affects our mood in a positive way and brings a sense of tranquility that helps us get through some difficult and stressful times. Although art may not be a vital necessity, no one can deny the joy it brings.

Art is also a great way to express ourselves and to translate the beauty in nature that surrounds us. And one of the best forms we can translate it into is a beautiful piece of drawing or painting. Inspiration is everywhere, all that is left for artists to do is to grab a medium and start recording it. To achieve optimal results, what better medium can we use than pastels!

Pastels offer extremely vivid and intense colors that can make your drawings look realistic when done skillfully. The sense of fulfillment you will feel while viewing your finished artwork is undeniable. With the right amount of passion, patience and determination, anyone can master the art of pastel drawing and be an inspiration to others.

To help you achieve just that, this book will provide you with some easy tips, techniques and tutorials that you will surely find beneficial for your development. So, grab your pastels and paper and bring out your artistic side. Now is the best time to show off your pastel drawing skills!

Thanks again for downloading this book, I hope you enjoy it!

Chapter 1: What is a Pastel?

A pastel is an art medium made by mixing pure powdered pigment together with a binder to create a thick paste. The thick paste is then formed into sticks and allowed to dry. Because they are fashioned with almost pure and dry pigment, the color produced by pastels is richer and more intense than that of other art media.

Pastel is also the term used to describe an artwork—can be a drawing or a painting—created using pastel sticks. A "pastelist" is an artist who uses pastels as their medium in creating their artwork.

1.1.   Types of Pastels

There are four general types of pastels: hard, soft, pencil, and oil. While they are all basically pigment in the form a stick, they differ in the way by which they are bound together. Hard pastels, soft pastels, and pastel pencils are held together with a water-based binder, usually a gum or resin. On the other hand, oil pastels are bound with an oil-based binder, usually oil or wax. This gives oil pastels a distinct texture comparable to oil paints.

Since hard, soft and pastel pencils are similarly bound, they are compatible with each other and can be worked on the same drawing or painting. Oil pastels, however, can only be worked with alone and cannot be combined with any other pastel types.

You can tell the distinction between these four pastel types by their look and texture.

Here are the main characteristics of each type:

Hard Pastels

Hard pastels contain less pigment and more binder than soft pastels. The more binder they have, the harder they become. This makes the color effect of hard pastels less intense. However, they do not crumble or crack as easily as soft pastels.

Hard pastels are usually cylindrical in shape and are hard and shiny. They can be sharpened using a knife to produce fine lines. Because they are firmer and more stable, hard pastels are particularly suitable for working on location and drawing techniques. Alternatively, the edges of hard pastel sticks can be used to apply extensive swathes of color.

Hard pastels are available in students' and artists' quality, and come in fewer colors than soft pastels. They can be used in blending, and are well-suited for working on small details, initial sketches and finishing touches.

Soft Pastels

Soft pastels, also called chalk pastels or "dry" pastels, are the most commonly used type of pastels. They have highly concentrated pigment that is bound together with the slightest amount of binder possible. The colors of soft pastels are delicately bright and intense. However, since they are dry and do not stick to the surface, they crumble easily and can be brushed off.

Soft pastels look and feel like typical blackboard chalk— soft and powdery with a cylindrical shape. This fragile consistency allows the artist to blend and layer various colors easily on the working surface. This also gives the artist prompt feedback on the colors as they apply them.

Soft pastels are best for beginners. If used with pastel pencils, soft pastels can help you create fine lines. As they are "chalky," you can make minor corrections or erasures which can be difficult to do with oil pastels.

With some manufacturers offering up to 500 colors, soft pastels have the widest selection of colors compared to other pastel types. They also come in a range of sizes: thick sticks, half sticks, and whole sticks.

Deciding between hard and soft pastels depends on the drawing techniques you'd like to make use of. If you're a beginner, you can begin mainly with soft pastels. Invest in a few individual hard pastels so you can try them out and use them for preliminary sketches and fine details.

Pastel Pencils

Pastel pencils are best if you want to create detailed and controlled artworks with pastels. They are versatile and can be used in combination with soft or hard pastels. You can use them wet or dry and they work well in blending technique. Pastel pencils can be sharpened to a point to draw precise and defined details. They are also recommended for basic sketching and drawing.

Pastel pencils look much like traditional pencils, but enclosed within the wood is a thin pastel stick with a consistency between soft and hard pastels. They are convenient to use as they are neat, unlike soft pastels. With pastel pencils, you can create quick sketches or drawings without much preparation or clean-up. This makes them suitable for working outdoors.

Oil Pastels

Oil pastels are like oil paints in terms of versatility and texture. But unlike oil paints, oil pastels don't have smelly chemicals and don't harden or dry out completely. As compared to soft pastels which produce more delicate and softer hue, oil pastels create brighter, more intense hue that makes them suitable for rough, bold and expressive work.

Oil pastels can also be worked, thinned, and diluted like oil paintings. They are round-shaped and have a wax-like, creamy consistency, making them easily distinguishable from soft pastels. They are also more stable and adhere to the working surface better than soft pastels.

Oil pastels do not require fixatives. They do not smudge, crumble, or release fine dust into the air which can result to respiratory irritation, whereas soft pastels often do. For this reason, and due to their non-toxic properties, oil pastels are the preferred type of pastel to be used in schools.

Oil pastels can also be great for beginners as it doesn't necessarily require setting up various solutions, brushes or other tools. All you need to get started are your oil pastel sticks and a sheet of paper to work on, and you're good to go.

Like other pastel types, oil pastels also come in either students' quality or artists' quality. Cheaper oil pastels have a look and feel like kids' crayons. They don't produce the same effect as artist quality pastels. This is frustrating to artists who are new to oil pastels and they often switch to other medium without discovering the real essence of oil pastels. So, if you're interested in trying out oil pastels, you need to be mindful of the difference between these two qualities. The difference alone could be the key factor in deciding whether you should continue using oil pastels.

1.2. Drawing Materials

To get started with pastel drawing, all you basically need is a set of pastels and a pastel paper to work on. However, due to the wide selections of drawing materials available on the market, a beginner can get confused and overwhelmed. To help you out, here is a list of art materials you need and some buying tips:

A Set of Pastels

Although there are many different choices available, choosing a set of pastel is quite easy. When you use pastels in drawing, you don't really want to blend individual colors too much as they tend to lose their brilliance or vibrancy if you do. So, in choosing a set of pastels, you would want to get the largest set you can afford to buy, with the most number of colors. This is to reduce the frequency of blending you would have to do.

Another factor to consider is how the colors are grouped in the various sets. Choosing a set really depends on your subject taste. Some sets are grouped with colors that would be used for purposes such as for drawing landscapes, portraits, seascapes, and the like. Some sets consist of general colors.

Pastel Paper

The paper you need to use for pastel drawing needs to have the required roughness (called the paper's "tooth") on which the pastel will adhere. The surface of an ordinary writing paper is too smooth and it doesn't allow the pastel to grip onto it. So, in buying paper for pastel drawing, always choose paper that is manufactured specifically for pastel work.

Pastel papers are fashioned in various ways to give different levels of texture and tooth. You can experiment with several pastel papers with varying textures and tooth until you find the one that suits your taste best.

Other Drawing Materials

While pastel sticks and paper are the basic materials you need in drawing, there are also other art materials you can make use of to aid in achieving better results.

- Charcoal sticks for preliminary sketches and drawings
- A clean cloth or wet wipes for cleaning up
- Sand paper for layered/textured drawings
- Gloves for skin protection
- Brushes for special effects and blending
- Bread for erasures
- Pastel stick holder
- Cotton buds to blend small areas
- A blending stump or a tissue to blend tones and colors
- Craft knife to trim paper to desired size and for special effects
- For other special effects, you may use a soft eraser, a sponge and toilet paper
- A can of fixative spray to protect your artwork and prevent it from being ruined by careless smudging (a hair spray can also be used as an alternative)

1.3.   Pastel Quality

Pastels, like other art media, come in different levels of quality. Generally, there are two main pastel grades: students' quality and artists' quality. Students' quality pastels are less expensive and usually have low quality pigments. They are also made with more binder and filler which make the colors less intense and vibrant. However, they do not easily crumble like artist grade pastels. Artists' quality pastels, on the other hand, contain stronger and more tightly-bound pigments. The pigment and binder are more proportional which makes the color bolder and more intense. Artists' quality pastels also have a wider selection of colors and are more fade-resistant than student grade pastels.

Beginners and intermediate artists who are not yet willing to invest in more expensive quality pastels can begin with the students' set. But if you are serious about pastel drawing, buy the artists' quality pastels and you will see a great difference with the results.

1.4.   Pastel Colors

You can blend pastel colors but you cannot mix them as well as you can with paint. To make up for this, a wide range of colors is made available on the market. You can purchase pastels individually or in sets. If you're a beginner and unsure as to which pastel type you want to invest in, you can begin by getting yourself individual pastels which will also keep your expenses low. Once you have figured which type you really want to buy, you can get a set of pastels that contains a good range of colors. You can also choose and customize your own set of colors.

Some artist grade pastels contain rare pigments which make them costlier than others. Alternatively, some student grade pastels contain artificial pigments which imitate the color of the more expensive natural pigments. If you see the word "hue" after the pigment name, it means that the pigment of the pastel is made using a cheaper substitute.

1.5.   Health and Safety

Pastels, especially soft pastels, are a dry medium and often deposit airborne dust which you can inhale as you work. This dust can cause respiratory discomfort and can be quite dangerous. To avoid inhaling pastel dust, work in a well-ventilated room. You can also wear face masks or get an air purifier to make you less exposed to dust.

Some pastels also contain toxic pigments like cadmium. Exposure to cadmium can lead to cadmium poisoning. To avoid this, buy only non-toxic pastels which are available at any local art supply store.

Chapter 2: Techniques for Pastel Drawing

The techniques for pastel drawing can be quite difficult to master especially for beginners. Unlike in painting, you cannot test the colors on a palette first before applying them to the surface, but rather you mix and blend the medium directly on the drawing surface. Also, en error in pastel drawing cannot be concealed the way an error in painting can be painted out.

Anyhow, there are various ways by which you can apply pastels to a surface. Some of these techniques can help you get away with errors. There is no right or wrong way in carrying out these techniques. You should simply select the technique that is most appropriate for your desired effect. For most pastel drawings, you can use these techniques in combination with each other.

2.1.   Blending

Blending is probably the most common and basic technique for pastel drawing. Blending happens when different pastel colors are applied in layers on the same area. You can smooth the transition between tones and colors by rubbing or smearing the pastel into the drawing surface. You can accomplish this using your finger, a tissue, blending stump, soft brush or cotton swab. You can use your finger for blending on large areas. But for smaller areas, use a blending stump or ear buds instead.

When you blend, and rub over the colors, you will notice that their vibrancy tends to diminish. Here is a way to overcome this: once you have blended the colors with your finger or a stump, gently rub the original colors on top of them to create a thin vibrant layer. This will help maintain the vibrancy of the pastel and achieve better results.

2.2.   Scumbling

Scumbling is a pastel technique in which thin but opaque layers of pastel are applied over the top of previously worked areas. This creates a partial covering and allows bits of the pastel underneath the new color to shine through. This technique produces visually stimulating results and is often used when working with landscapes and other natural scenes and objects.

When scumbling is done, the overlapping colors visually "mix" and cause the viewer to perceive a new color. This is often referred to as *optical color mixing*. For instance, if blue streaks are applied next to, or over yellow streaks, it creates a perception of green.

As you have imagined, the tooth or texture of the paper is one of the factors that affect the process of scumbling. So, to achieve the desired effect of scumbling, consider the tooth or texture of the paper that you will use.

2.3. Stippling

Stippling is a common drawing technique used to create areas of light and shade by dotting the medium down onto the working surface. This process is repeated until the desired effect is created. The more compressed the dots are, the darker the area will be. This technique works well in painting as well as in pastel drawing. It can also be done with other drawing media such as charcoal, crayons, and conte crayons.

Stippling can create an optical illusion when done by a skilled artist. From a distant view, the areas in which the shading was created will look like a smooth application of pastels. The dots will only be apparent when surveyed very closely.

2.4. Hatching

Hatching has 6 basic forms: *parallel hatching*, *contour hatching*, *cross hatching*, *fine cross hatching*, *tick hatching*, and *woven hatching*. Hatching techniques are used to create value, texture and the optical illusion of light and form by drawing lines close together in similar or various directions. Aside from pastels, these linear techniques also work well with many other drawing media such as colored pencils, graphite, and pen and ink. Hatching can also be observed in traditional techniques for printmaking such as engraving and etching.

Parallel Hatching

Parallel hatching is a basic form of hatching that uses non-crossing lines to demonstrate the value (light and shadow) on or round an object in a drawing. Hatching consists of sets of parallel lines positioned closely together. The areas where you place hatching will appear shaded and darker, and the areas where you don't will give the impression of a featured highlight.

Contour Hatching

Instead of using simple parallel lines, it is sometimes necessary to curve the lines and adhere to the contours of an object. This is referred to as *contour hatching*. In addition to creating value, contour hatching technique also enhances the volume and dimensionality of the object you are drawing.

Cross Hatching

After drawing one set of lines, you may add another set of lines on top to add more value to your hatching. The second set of lines can be drawn diagonally or perpendicularly to the first set, and can be another set of parallel lines of curved lines to adhere to the contours of the object. This cross-hatching technique is an effective way to create density variations and to deepen the values in your drawing.

Fine Cross Hatching

Fine cross hatching is the richest and most delicate hatching technique. It is done using the same method as above, consisting of various layers of cross hatching instead of only two, to create more gradations in value and tone. In fine cross hatching, a fine-line pencil or the edge of a hard-pastel stick is best used to draw more detailed and precise lines that will seem to blend together when viewed from far away.

Tick Hatching

Tick hatching is composed of short parallel marks or "ticks" that are piled over one another to produce variations in density. This technique works best with a broader pen or pastel to enhance the graphic quality of your drawing.

Woven Hatching

Woven hatching is also referred to as *basket hatching*. This technique provides very striking effects and enhances the graphic quality of your work when done correctly. To do this technique, draw a short set of parallel lines in the same direction, then another set of parallel lines in an almost-perpendicular or diagonal direction. The effect of this technique will look woven (thus the name) when used correctly. The marks can also be cross-hatched to create more density and achieve your desired effect.

2.5. Scratching

The technique of scratching gives your drawings added details that are simple but unique. To do this, lay down two or more contrasting colors before doing the main drawing. The greater the number of colors you lay, the greater the range of colors that will be revealed upon scratching. The result is more effective if the color of the final layer on top is dark. To do the scratching part, you need to make use of a scratching tool. It can be a needle, a painting knife, or a comb. If you don't have any of these tools, you can also sharpen your pastel stick to a point and use it to scratch out the image.

2.6. Feathering

Feathering is a drawing technique that usually uses layers of short strokes that may overlap or cross on top of each other. The lines that are drawn may also curve to adhere to the contours of an object in your drawing, and this adds to the illusion of light and form. Like scumbling, feathering can also provide vibrancy to your work, and result to optical color mixing in which the colors are visually mixed instead of being physically blended on the drawing surface.

This technique is particularly good for providing the glistening appearance of feathers, scales, and fabric, or for creating effects that are distinctive with light.

2.7. Other Tips and Techniques

There are three ways to use a pastel: by drawing with the end, the edge, or the side. Hold the pastel stick as you would hold a pen or pencil and it will create a great expression that suggests a sense of the gesticulation you made. You can vary the breadth of the line by applying alternate pressure to the pastel. The more pressure you apply, the more pastel you will be laying down on the surface. To create thinner lines, apply the pastel more lightly on the paper or you can also use the edge of the stick.

For detail work, you can create finer lines using the sharp edge of a new pastel stick. When it becomes blunt through use, you can re-sharpen it with a cutter or knife. You can also reshape the pastel stick by scraping it against a rough surface such as sandpaper. While most artists use pastel pencils to create more precise lines, learning this technique helps especially when you don't have a pencil available and need to draw finer marks.

If you want to create broad streaks of color quickly, you can draw with the side of the stick. For better results, split the stick in two and use one half of it. Alter the pressure to produce varying gradations of texture on the paper. When the side of the stick has eroded due to constant use, it will leave two sharp edges which you can then use to draw finer lines.

As previously mentioned, you can use a combination of any of these techniques in the same drawing. It is necessary to incorporate various strokes and marks in any image. Regardless of which technique/s you use, the goal is to always create established layers of various colors on the pastel paper. This provides depth in your work and enhances the illusion of light and form. Practice these easy techniques to further develop your artistic skills and to create successful pieces of pastel artwork.

Chapter 3: Basic Tips and Tutorials

Pastels can be a challenging medium to master. Their loose characteristic makes it difficult to control on the drawing surface. For this reason, beginners are often discouraged that they tend to dismiss this medium after only a few tries and move on to something else. This is unfortunate as many new artists miss out on the opportunity of discovering how great pastels can be. They shun the medium that might have been perfect for them if only they worked with it a little longer.

So, if you're new to pastels, keep working and don't limit yourself. Pastel drawing can be fulfilling. You can even discover new techniques of your own as you move along. Having said that, here are some basic tutorials, as well as some tips, to get you started with the amazing world of pastel drawing.

3.1. Landscapes

One of the most common subjects of artists for their drawings are landscapes, and it is no wonder. As artists, we are moved by the natural beauty that surrounds us and interpreting them into beautiful works of art is the least we can do. Landscapes are overflowing with interesting shapes, lines, and varied colors. These elements often arrange themselves into visually appealing compositions and the artist will simply need to record them in the form of a drawing or a painting.

Pastels are inherently loose which makes them the perfect medium for interpreting natural sceneries such as landscapes. In this tutorial, we will record a typical, natural landscape with the use of soft pastels. Work on an orange pastel paper that has a rough texture (tooth) as this tutorial calls for heavy layering. The heavy tooth of the surface allows you to apply multiple layers of color without upsetting the tooth. This is essential for the coherent reception of the material.

Moving on, here are the steps in creating a beautiful landscape artwork:

- To begin, work a layer of darker blue over a layer of lighter blue pastels. This will form the background of the landscape. The light blue pastel creates the outlines for the clouds and develops the transition from light to dark. Use your finger to gently blend the colors of the clouds.

- Create a line for the distant row of trees. This should overlap the background. Apply a dark yellow-green pastel to begin. Then apply burnt umber followed by a light mark of black. Blend the colors gently with your finger and leave a hard edge on top of the row of trees.

- Next, to form the distant ground, use a variety of yellow-greens, followed by yellow-ochre, light cream, and a few bands of Burnt Sienna. This creates shapes of color that are aligned horizontally.

- Add several distant trees. Do not worry about the details. Instead, focus on the values, shapes and colors that are created.

- Apply a fair amount of light cream into the middle ground and allow tiny portions of the orange pastel paper to show through. Apply a few bands of burnt sienna for added color.

- Still working on the middle ground, apply patches of red over layers of purple, then darken it with burnt umber. This will form the grasses for the landscape. Use dark yellow-green pastel to draw smaller grasses and highlight it with a lighter yellow-green.

- Continue adding some more details to the image such as formations of rocks with small trees and bits of grass behind them. As you reach the closer ground or the foreground, make the lines for the grass longer and more precise. Use different colors and create variations in value to make your drawing appear more animated.

- Draw additional strokes with light cream pastel to imply the field of grass. Leave some recesses to reveal portions of the darker layers' underneath. You can also use a lighter cream pastel to highlight the tips of the taller grass blades.

- Going back to the background, grab a white pastel to intensify the colors of the clouds. Gently blend the new colors with the previously applied colors using your finger.

Your landscape drawing is now complete! You can finish off your work by spraying fixative all over it. You can also use a hairspray as an alternative. Fixative spray protects your work and prevents it from smudging.

3.2. Seascapes

Your repertoire as an artist will not be complete if you are not able to draw seascapes. This subject matter can be tricky as oceans are continually moving and your drawing needs to capture that illusion for it to be successful. Additionally, it can be quite difficult to draw if your target is always moving.

If you're a beginner, you can start with an image reference as an alternative. Learn and understand the basics of creating the illusion of waves and you can draw them easily. For seascapes, the same with landscapes, it is recommended to use a surface that has a heavy tooth as this subject often requires substantial applications of layering. You can use soft, hard or oil pastels, depending on your preference. As you move along, apply these tips to achieve appealing and desirable results:

- Scrutinize the subject very closely and you will be able to identify the directional lines, as well as the colors, values and tones being used. These elements are all essential to create the effect you are after. Place colors and values in the right locations within your drawing to give the viewer the illusion that they are seeing actual waves.

- Consider the sequence in which you are to draw the subject. Typically, pastelist commence the drawing by working on the background. Then develop the middle ground and foreground over the accomplished background. In this manner, you will be able to layer the colors in a more effective way.

- Create a great extent of value (the lightness and shadiness of a color) within your drawing. Value plays a vital role in the way we perceive things. Use different tones and shades from the same color group and it will help you achieve the illusion you're trying to make. For instance: although the ocean is generally blue, use other tones such as blue-green, green, dark blue, light blue and so on. Layer these colors and their values and it will aid in creating the illusion of moving water.

- Another important factor to consider is the directional lines. Since we are working with waves, observe the contrast between horizontal and diagonal lines. These are examples of contour lines for which you can use the layering techniques you have learned so far.

- Apply your medium in a manner that it adheres to the curves and contours which characterize the subject. Work with the contours of the waves to effectively bring about the effect you're after.

Due to its simplicity and seemingly unvarying color, the ocean might look like a simple thing to draw. But the challenge is to capture the illusion of movement and gleam of the waves within your drawing, and drive the viewer into believing that the waves are moving. With a little practice and enhancement of skills, you will eventually be able to pull it off quite easily.

3.3. Clouds

Another basic subject that a pastelist should master is the clouds. Landscapes and other scenes often require the presence of the sky. While a cloudless and still sky is easier to accomplish, —only some basic blending and layering of the medium will be enough—a scene that calls for clouds can become more complicated. Here are few useful tips to help you create more realistic-looking clouds.

- When you are drawing clouds, the first thing you should remember is that clouds are three-dimensional objects. Consequently, they will often have a shaded part and a highlighted part. It is essential to create the illusion of shadows and highlights to produce more natural and realistic clouds.

- Clouds take on various forms and shapes. This gives you the freedom to be loose and diverse when you're making the outlines of the marks. Exercise this freedom as this will promote the illusion and effect of organic shapes.

- As with most subject matters, it is important to observe value. Endeavor to incorporate a greater extent of value in any of your drawings. As clouds are often blue and white, you can use other tones such as gray, dark blue, light blue and the like, to create the illusion of three-dimensionality and dynamism.

These tips are important to remember not only for clouds, but for all types of subject matters. Apply these tips and in no time, you will master the creation of realistic-looking clouds.

Landscapes, seascapes and clouds may seem basic, but pulling them off convincingly requires skills and thorough understanding of the art. Exercise your creativity and adroitness in every artwork you are working on. With a good selection of medium and application of techniques, you can turn from a novice pastelist to a competent and skillful artist.

Chapter 4: Portrait Drawing with Pastels

Portrait drawing is a traditional art form. After all, what better subject can an artist have but themselves and the people around them? Whether you're drawing a self-portrait, a portrait of a loved one, or a stranger's perhaps, there are two main factors you should be mindful about: the proportions of the human face and the accuracy of your drawing to those proportions. In this chapter, we will study the basic rules of symmetry for the human face, which all pastelist, painters and artists alike must learn and understand. The other sections will provide you with simple approaches to drawing realistic eyes, nose, lips and ears.

4.1. Understanding Facial Proportions

Drawing a portrait is rather like drawing any other types of subject matter. You must scrutinize the subject so that you can draw the features accurately. The goal is to always make the closest resemblance possible between the portrait and the subject. To do this, it is important to understand facial proportions first.

Proportion is the relation of one part to another or to the whole with respect to placement and size. Generally, human faces follow the same rules of symmetry but many people still make mistakes when drawing the human face due to their lack of understanding of the facial symmetry. When drawing a face, follow these basic rules to get the job done correctly:

- First thing to keep in mind is that the eyes are always found in the middle of the face. People tend to make mistakes on this and incorrectly position the eyes way up the forehead. You can draw a horizontal line halfway in the middle of the face to serve as the "eye line" and position the eyes there.

- Typically, the width of a human face is five times the width of a single eye. Of course, you need to draw only two eyes. The concept of "five eyes" should serve as a guide to help you determine the correct width of the face.

- When drawing a line for the nose, it should run from the center of the eye line down to the bottom of the face. When drawing the actual nose, it should be thinnest between the eyes and growing a bit wider down the nostrils. There are exceptions to this, of course. Obviously, everyone has a unique nose. Some noses are longer, some are wider, some are thinner, and so on. So, you really need to pay attention to the details of your subject's nose to capture it more accurately.

- Each inside corner of the eyes typically aligns with either edge of the nose, while each pupil of the eyes typically aligns with either corner of the mouth.

43

- The line for the mouth runs from the center of the nose line down the bottom of the face. This line indicates the location where the top and bottom lip meet.

- Typical ears are positioned between the nose line and the eye line.

Keep these simple basics in mind and use them as a guide to help you draw a properly proportioned face. Most importantly, study the face of your subject carefully to get more precise results. These are only standard rules that may be applicable to most people, but not to everyone.

4.2. Drawing the Eye

As the saying goes, eyes are the windows to the soul. Amongst all facial features, the eyes are the most expressive. When you're drawing the subject's eyes, it will be more convincing if you can resemble not only the physical characteristics of the eyes but also the emotions that may hide behind them. To draw an eye that looks realistic, here is a step-by-step approach:

- To begin, sketch the outlines of the shape of the eye using a skin-tone color first, then a dark brown.

- Layer the colors in the iris of the eye. Apply green, blue, and a bit of yellow then blend the colors with your finger.

- Next, layer the darker values and tones of the iris over the initial colors. You can use blue and dark brown for this. Layering is always essential in any drawing. It creates depth and makes the colors look more convincing and realistic.

- Apply additional colors directly upon the darker layer, but this time, less mixing and smudging is needed. You can use light blue and yellow-green for this.

- Highlight some of the areas in the iris part of the eye with a light cream. You can also use this color in the white areas of the eyes.

- Apply some marks with red, cream, and red-orange. This is to indicate the edges of the eye.

- Layer white on top of the slightly darker values of the white areas of the eye. This creates a highlight and makes the eye look moist. You can also use white on top of the iris to make it look "sparkly."

- Apply skin-tone colors round the eye. Work the colors into the surface as you apply them.

- Continue to add and blend the skin-tone colors into the working surface.

- Finally, add the eyelashes with a black pencil. A nicely sharpened pastel pencil will create more precise-looking eyelashes.

Your realistic eye drawing is now complete! As always, a careful study of your subject's facial features should be done to make the finished work more accurate.

4.3. Drawing the Nose

Drawing noses is easier than you may think. Many people seem to struggle with this part but it's rather simple. Here are the basics:

- To begin, draw four curved lines: two lines for the nostrils, two lines for the edges of the nose.

- Apply darker values on the shaded areas of the nose. Begin with the darkest areas then to the midtones. You can do this with a pencil first.

- Continue to add shading on the right locations of the nose to make the illusion that there is a source of light. Do not add more marks or lines. Focus on shading the dark areas while leaving some of the areas slightly untouched.

- Adding more value will make your nose look more realistic. Light areas of the nose will appear protruded, while the dark areas will look like they're way at the back.

- Look for the light and dark areas on your subject's nose and draw them as you see them. By doing this, your nose will appear lifelike.

Isn't that easy? All you need to draw are four simple lines and the rest is shading and adding value. As for the shape, size and length of the nose, it really depends on your subject. There is no specific formula when it comes to drawing noses, you should observe your subject closely and draw the specifications that you will see.

4.4. Drawing the Lips

Some people seem to have problems when it comes to drawing the lips or mouth. This is mainly because everyone has a unique set of lips. So, there is no definite method for drawing the lips but there are some things you can consider that may make the task easier.

- Observation is the key. Every set of lips is different. Whether your subject is a live person or from a photo reference, it is always important to scrutinize each feature to get the exact size, shape, color and curves of the lips.

- Use contour lines to aid in outlining the shape of the lips. Also, apply the layering techniques you have learned from the previous chapters to make the lips look believable. Apply the pastels onto the working area using contour lines, as well.

- At the beginning, it is okay to be loose with your drawing. Forming the shape of the lips might call for some mistakes and that is fine, so long as you get the correct form. Especially when you're using soft pastels, you can remedy the mistakes later. Keep your working area clean but do not worry too much about stray lines and marks.

- Pastel drawing requires several layering, particularly with soft pastels. You may need to do more layering to get the result that you want so don't get frustrated if your work doesn't look developed enough after only a few layers. Establish the colors and always keep your cool.

4.5.   Drawing the Ears

As with all facial features, ears vary in sizes and shapes. Pay close attention to the shapes and lines of your subject's ears and draw them exactly as you see them. Drawing realistic ears is simple. You only need to draw the outlines or contours of your subject's ears and the rest is shading and adding value (same as with drawing noses). As there is no definite formula regarding drawing ears, remember these basic tips instead to accomplish the job more effectively:

- Be familiar with the proper location of the ears. As discussed earlier, ears are typically positioned between the nose line and the eye line. Be careful not to place them way below the nose or way above the eyes as they will not look properly proportioned if you do.

- Keep in mind that every set of ears is unique, as all facial features are. Learn to analyze and examine even the subtlest details that are present on every subject and from every angle. Little details can make a difference with the outcome.

- Remember that ears are complementary features of the portrait—they are not the main subject. Sometimes, the ears are completely or partially covered either by the subject's hair or any other accessory the subject may be wearing. Do not become too preoccupied with working with the ears that you overlook the whole picture.

Drawing the facial features often follow the same basic rules. And in all your drawings, never miss to observe each feature of your subject's face to capture its unique specifics.

Hopefully by now you have already drawn a realistic portrait with all the facial features properly positioned. As you will notice, one great thing about the pastel medium is that it gives the artists the best of both worlds. Although we generally call it "drawing," the results often look like they are "painted" instead of drawn. This is due to the vivid and vibrant colors that pastels often contain. In fact, pastel-drawn artworks are usually called "painting."

Now that you have learned the basics of portrait drawing with pastels, why don't you invite a friend or a loved one to become the subject for your drawings? A truly skillful artist can not only draw a good portrait that resembles the subject, but can also capture the character and personality of the subject in their drawings. Now this may sound too demanding but with a creative mind and passionate will, the possibilities are limitless!

Chapter 5: An Overview of Still Life Drawing

Although it may not always be the most interesting subject, drawing still life can be quite exciting. It is good practice for developing and enhancing observational skills, as well as interpretative skills of an artist. With still life, you can learn how to perceive objects like an artist—with a mindful awareness of their shape, tone, texture, color, form, outline, proportions and composition.

5.1. What is Still Life?

But what really is still life? To say simply, still life is an arrangement or a scene of inanimate objects that are either painted or drawn from observation. Still life arrangement can be composed of related or unrelated objects. The goal is to create an artwork that is skillfully constructed, thought provoking and aesthetically pleasing.

Contrary to landscape painting or drawing, still life subjects give artists more freedom to create the picture and decide on its compositions before painting or drawing anything. Traditionally, objects that comprise still life arrangements include foods, flowers, glasses, bottles and vases. Some modern artists, however, have averted from tradition and they are more liberated in choosing their subjects.

5.2. The Rule of Odds

The Rule of Odds applies to all forms of visual arts—photography, sculpture, graphic design and painting. This rule states that objects grouped together will look more interesting and appealing if they have an odd number. Viewers, for some reason, would rather look at a composition of "3" objects instead of "2," or "5" rather than "4."

The human eye has the tendency to wander to the middle of the group. If it sees an even number of objects, it will end up looking at the blank center and this inhibits eye movement.

When composing a still life arrangement, strive to apply the Rule of Odds to achieve a more aesthetically pleasing composition. If you have one main object, complement it with two or four supporting objects so one of them will be the center.

Pastel Drawing: 1-2-3 Easy Techniques To Mastering Pastel Drawing

Still life has given artists a platform to explore their association with the objects that exist in their world. Practice drawing with still life objects to improve your techniques and further develop your skills as an artist.

Conclusion

Thank you again for downloading this book!

I hope this book could unleash the artist in you and inspire you to become a better, more competent pastel list.

The possibilities with respect to creating art are seemingly endless! In our world filled with beauty and wonder, you will never run out of inspiration. The marvelous scenes of nature, the picturesque views of our surroundings, and the smiles of our loved ones are all too inciting not to draw and capture every moment of.

But art isn't only about interpreting the world in which we live in. It is also a great way to express our inner thoughts and feelings about life. Our dreams, memories, longings, fears and joy can also be translated into wondrous artworks. Art is a means of self-expression that lets the audience peek into the world within us. What a nice feeling it is when you can just let everything out!

Everywhere we go, art is evident, inspiring us in many ways, influencing us to become a better person. It is amazing to know that with only a piece of paper in hand and a simple medium such as a pastel, we can pay tribute to all the beautiful things that life has given us, in a creative and passionate way.

Now, the next step is to keep moving forward. Practice your pastel drawing skills and never be afraid to take it to the next level. If at first you don't achieve the result that you want, do not dwell on the frustration and do better next time. A pastel drawing master was once a beginner who failed but didn't give up. Keep pushing yourself to the limit. Do not hold back. Be bolder. Let your creativity overflow. Who knows, you might just one day be lined up with all the world's greatest pastel artists!

Finally, if you enjoyed this book, please take the time to share your thoughts and post a review on Amazon. It'd be greatly appreciated!

Thank you and good luck!

www.ingramcontent.com/pod-product-compliance
Lightning Source LLC
Chambersburg PA
CBHW061226180526
45170CB00003B/1173